Fast Track Your Career:
Three Steps for Finding Work You Love

By Markell R. Steele, M.Ed.
1st Edition

Futures in Motion, Inc.
P.O. Box 14633
Belmont Shore, CA 90853
www.futures-in-motion.com
(877) 210-3252
info@futures-in-motion.com

Copyright 2007 © by Markell R. Steele

ISBN 978-0-6151-5870-9

All rights reserved. No part of this book may be reproduced in whole or in part, by electronic or any other means which exist or may yet be developed, without permission from the publisher.

Fast Track Your Career: Three Steps for Finding Work You Love

Table of Contents

4 Welcome Message from Markell

5 Introduction

7 Part One: Gaining Personal Insight
Chapter One - Introduction to Career Planning
Chapter Two - Find Meaning in Your Career
Chapter Three - Discover What You're Good At

35 Part Two: Getting a Reality Check
Chapter Four - Find Good Career Information

45 Part Three: Charting Your Career Path
Chapter Five - Learn How to Get Ahead
Chapter Six - Plan for Next Steps
Chapter Seven - Plan to Succeed

60 A Few Concluding Thoughts

61 Career Information Resources

62 About Futures In Motion, Inc.

63 About The Author

Welcome to Fast Track Your Career:
Three Steps for Finding Work You Love!

The secret to enjoying a satisfying career is to carefully plan your career path. Whether you're new to the job market or you're a mid-career professional, it's never too late.

My career guide includes everything you need to start on the path toward uncovering your passion. It includes an overview of the career-planning process and tools to assess your core values, identify your key skills, and set effective career goals. I've worked with hundreds of clients who have found satisfying careers by using the process outlined on these pages.

In each chapter I'll explain important career-planning concepts and walk you through exercises to apply the concepts to your personal career situation. At the end of this guide I've included information on resources that you can use for further exploration and planning.

Each chapter builds on the previous one, so take one step at a time and complete the chapters in sequence. If you've downloaded this career guide, I suggest that you create a folder to save the career guide and your completed exercises.

As you approach career planning, keep an open mind about the possibilities. With careful thought and diligent action, you'll have a great start toward finding work that you love. Congratulations on taking the first step.

You are about to embark on an exciting journey!

To Your Success!

Markell Steele

Markell R. Steele, M.Ed., Owner
Futures in Motion, Inc.

Introduction

How I Found a Career That I Love

When I took up career counseling as my profession of choice, I was so excited about the possibilities. In my first positions, I worked as a "generalist." I was expected to work with any client who walked through the door, in addition to delivering workshops on an assortment of career-planning topics. During my work with clients, we addressed everything from choosing a major, changing careers and preparing for graduate school, to job search preparation, resume writing and interviewing skills. I counseled college freshman, college seniors, graduate students, and experienced professionals across the spectrum of jobs. I did it all! I was really good at this, too. The clients with the most complex career concerns were often referred to me. I was recognized for my ability to help people feel confident about their career options.

At first I enjoyed the variety, but eventually I began to feel like I wasn't helping people build a solid foundation for career success and satisfaction. While I loved being a career counselor, I felt like something was missing.

Then I had an opportunity to participate in a management development program offered by my organization's human resources department. By that time, I had already decided I was ready to move on. I wasn't really sure where I should go or when I would make the move, so I applied for and was accepted into the program. In preparation for the kick-off retreat, we were asked to complete a few self-assessment exercises. As we were being debriefed on the results, I realized that there were so many aspects of being a career counselor that I hadn't considered, such as the type of clients I would most enjoy working with, the setting that would be the best fit, and what exactly I would want my clients to achieve.

Throughout the weekend I continued to get confirmation that I was in the wrong place. It was an "a-ha" moment. Now, it all made sense!

The reason I had felt so frustrated and out of place was because I was in the wrong environment. I wasn't motivated by the same things as my colleagues were so the environment didn't support me. I realized that my values weren't in sync with people who thrive in that environment. I also realized that while I had well-developed counseling skills, there were many more skills I wanted to use. For example, I love marketing, but the organization already had a marketing person. I love connecting people to career opportunities, but there was already an employer-relations person. One option was to become a department director, but I wasn't interested in "playing the game" to advance in that setting.

After a little soul-searching, career research, and personal preparation, I decided to make my move toward establishing a private career counseling practice. I started Futures in Motion, Inc. in 2002, and have organized the company around helping professionals design career paths based on what will bring them the highest levels of career satisfaction and success.

By evaluating my career and aspirations, clarifying my most important values, identifying my "motivated skills," and goal-setting, I decided that my dreams could become a reality and set about making it so. While it did take some work and patience, almost every day since I had my "a-ha" moment has been joyful. People ask me all the time how I found a career that is so satisfying, so I have had plenty of chances to share my story and the secrets to my success.

I'm so happy to share them with you now. Let's jump right in!

PART ONE

GAINING PERSONAL INSIGHT

Fast Track Your Career: Three Steps for Finding Work You Love

Introduction to Career Planning

The Importance Of Career Planning

You've probably recognized that the world of work has changed dramatically. The changes have forced many people to re-evaluate their career progress and the way they approach career advancement. You'll continue to see shifts brought about by increased economic competition, the technology explosion, and changing demographics. While there are no guarantees, you'll have a better chance of keeping up with the inevitable changes in the job market if you develop a solid career plan and implement career management strategies.

What makes the new world of work different? In years past, you could enjoy relative job security without the threat of technological advancements or global competition. You could start your career at a company and, through a series of predictable advancements, move easily into a supervisor or management position and settle in. As the economic landscape changed in the early 1990s, companies responded by flattening their ranks and extending their talent searches beyond the United States. Employers then had to compete as they never had to before. Meanwhile, employees were expected to be functional specialists whereas in the past, they were highly valued just for being a competent manager. Today, as companies grapple with the challenge of keeping up with technological innovations, they expect nearly all employees to be savvy about technology.

All of these changes have forced employees to adopt new ways to thrive in the world of work. One significant change is that people are responding to these pressures by adopting a proactive attitude toward managing their career. They're being more strategic and realizing that there are many factors to consider when making a good career choice, including identifying their strongest skills, and determining what role they'd like to play, where they'd like to work, and what type of education or training they'd need to complete.

I've also found that satisfied professionals understand the world of work and the nature of the job market. They realize that there will always be cycles of job creation and job elimination. They understand who they are and how they want their personality and values to be reflected in their careers.

Get on the right path

And, they're committed to doing what it takes to make things happen in their careers. Of course they didn't gain all of this wisdom overnight. By getting involved in the career-planning process they learned how to move closer to their career goals.

What is career planning?

Career planning will help you make sense of a complex work world. It's so easy to get overwhelmed by a seemingly endless array of career options and career opportunities. By taking an in-depth look at what you really want to accomplish in your career, you'll be able to cut through the clutter to create a career that is personally meaningful.

When I begin working with a new client, I emphasize that career planning is a continuous, life-long process. It helps you identify strengths and growth areas, decide on a direction, and stick with it even when you feel overwhelmed by a lot of possibilities. Career planning also helps you define a purpose for your career and life. And finally, it gives you the tools to explore all the qualities that make you who you are, and integrate those qualities into a satisfying life.

I use this four-phase career-planning process:

> *Phase One. Assess Your Situation* to determine what you need in your career to be satisfied. Analyze your values, motivated skills, personality characteristics, interests, and lifestyle preferences.
>
> *Phase Two. Explore the Possibilities* to identify careers that are best suited to your personal attributes and preferences. Learn how to use the best sources of career information to identify options that will meet your goals.
>
> *Phase Three. Decide on a Career Direction* after evaluating your options. Learn decision-making strategies to pinpoint a career target.
>
> *Phase Four. Develop and Implement a Personalized Plan* to successfully connect with your career target and expand your professional network. Create a powerful resume, cover letter, and other support materials. Fine-tune your interviewing and networking skills.

This career guide takes you through Phase One and Phase Two of the process. You'll develop an enhanced understanding of how to bring all aspects of your life into alignment and meet the challenges of the new world of work. Once you're equipped with the necessary tools, you'll be armed with strategies and methods to use as you begin your career and in times of transition.

As I mentioned earlier, I've not only guided many people through this process, I've completed it myself. You're not alone if you feel uncomfortable while trying to take an objective look at your career progress, your personal attributes, and your aspirations. You may begin to doubt that you can really take your career where you want it to go. You may even wonder how you made it this far.

I wrote this career guide to help you regain a sense of hope, passion, and purpose for what lies ahead. This may be a difficult journey. It will require a lot of work on your part. I encourage you to meet the challenge head-on and keep an open mind. Your perseverance will be rewarded.

You now have a better understanding of how people plan their careers. Next, we'll explore how and where people get meaning in their life and career.

Regain a sense of hope, passion and purpose

Find Meaning in Your Career

Seasons and Reasons

As you move through various stages in life, your values often shift. During adolescence and the early stages of adulthood, most of us focus on establishing our independence. We want to prove ourselves as adults and are likely to seek out opportunities to display our competence.

In our thirties, we begin to re-evaluate our life and career. We wonder if we've set off on the right path and if things will turn out the way we had hoped. It can be a stressful time, but most of us settle in and move forward.

There does come a stage in life, generally in the late-thirties to mid-forties, when we seriously consider our progress in our life and career. This is a time when people begin to wonder if they will ever achieve what they envisioned for their lives or whether their achievements so far really mean anything. It's at this stage that many people begin exploring dormant interests. You might take up competitive athletics, increase your participation in community organizations or go back to school.

Some people describe "hitting their stride" when they move past that stage. They have more confidence than ever in their abilities, are at peace with their life decisions and career choices, and are ready for a satisfying future. Generally, their career is at its' peak, and they're performing at the highest levels.

Each of us is motivated differently. Our motivations are rooted in the meaning we attach to certain desired outcomes of our cumulative actions, or by achieving the goals we set for ourselves. In this chapter, we'll discuss the role our values play in determining what we strive for in our career and life, how we go about getting what we want, and how we apply our values in everyday situations and when making major decisions. We'll also discuss the SMART way to set goals, and strategies for making effective decisions.

Each of us is motivated differently

Purpose and Motivation

If you're like most people, your life feels the most meaningful when you have a big-picture perspective of how your everyday activities fit into a larger puzzle. This broad perspective helps you stay focused and gives you a sense of purpose. When you're focused it's easier to figure out which activities will get you closer to your goals.

When psychologist Abraham Maslow set out to simplify the research on how people are motivated, he found that, contrary to conventional wisdom at the time, people are motivated to satisfy either growth or deficiency needs. And, it's not until a fundamental need is met that a person will strive for growth. So, for example, in the hierarchy of needs, the need for more responsibility or recognition won't be a significant motivator until a person has met his need for food and shelter.

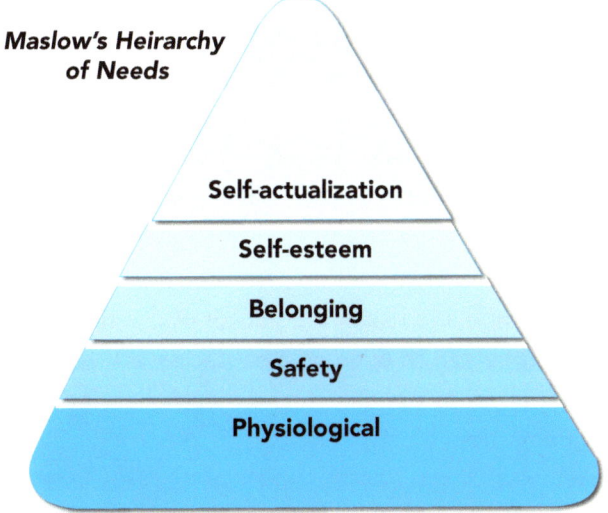

How Our Needs Affect Us

Another layer of insight came from psychologist and organizational culture expert Edgar Schein. He found that people generally find meaning in activities at different stages in their careers, based on a combination of eight career anchors. As we progress in our careers, we begin to develop a self-concept that enables us to answer questions about our skills, competencies, and motivations. We also become better at judging our performance and organizational fit. However, according to Schein's findings, many people aren't clear about what is truly important to them and therefore often make career decisions that aren't as satisfying as they could be. Schein identified eight key motivators, or career anchors, that underlie most career decisions. By looking at a series of decisions and analyzing the underlying motivators, they can determine the most prevalent motivators at various points in time.

Self-actualization — In this stage, when all other needs are satisfied, we're motivated to do what we're meant to do.

Self-esteem — In this stage, we're motivated by a need for self-respect and to be respected by others. We want to feel confident and valued as a person.

Belonging — In this stage, we're motivated by a need to affiliate with others and find a place where we can be accepted as part of a group.

Safety — In this stage, we're motivated to satisfy our need for a safe, secure environment, and the sense that we're free from harm.

Physiological — In this stage a person is motivated to satisfy biological needs at the most basic level, such as food, water, and air.

The 8 Career Anchors:

Technical/Functional Competence — value being perceived as very knowledgeable, as producing high-quality work, often in a specialized field. People with this anchor identify strongly with their expertise and like the recognition that comes with their ability to succeed in their chosen arena.

General Management Competence — value advancement to higher levels of responsibility as well as opportunities for leadership, making a greater impact on the organization, and high income potential. People with this anchor often display competence in the three areas of management: analytical, interpersonal, and emotional.

Autonomy/Independence — value having the flexibility to do things in their own way and independent of others whenever possible. This group prefers environments that allow them to achieve through their own efforts. They often feel restricted in traditional organizational structures that require a great deal of interdependency.

Security/Stability — value long-term employment with a company including consistent salary and some career progression. People with this anchor tend to identify strongly with the organization's mission and goals.

Entrepreneurial Creativity — value challenge and risk in the pursuit of creating new business. People with this anchor are motivated to overcome obstacles, are willing to step into the unknown, and have a desire for personal gain and recognition for what they have achieved outside of an organization.

Service/Dedication to a Cause — value serving others through a variety of activities. Individuals with this anchor are motivated to provide support, comfort, and education, or generally improve the lives of others.

Pure Challenge — value winning and being challenged at high levels. People in this group strive to be the best, be the first, and to surpass previous achievements.

Lifestyle Integration — value a life based on a balanced pursuit of career, interests, time with family and friends, hobbies, leisure activities, and travel, etc. For people with this anchor, work and career are not their major source of identity.

The exercise that follows is designed to help you understand your motivations by analyzing your career progress, aspirations, and career anchors over time. You'll look at the key decisions you've made in your life and career to date, and determine which anchors were in effect. This will help you see patterns in your decision-making and how your anchors have impacted your career progress and satisfaction.

Career Lifeline

Step One: Use the grid below or take out a blank piece of paper (8.5x11 or 8.5x14) and draw the grid.

Step Two: Add key events or milestones in your life and career, in chronological order. Examples can include birth, first day of school, first job, high school graduation, beginning college, getting married, graduation from college, first big promotion, etc. Include whatever events have been significant to you.

Step Three: Next, look into the future and write down key events you would like to see occur.

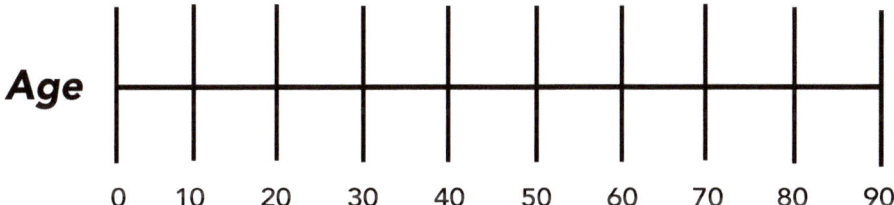

Questions for Reflection

In the space below, take some time to reflect on the milestones you indicated on your **Career Lifeline**.

What were the anchors at those points?

What pattern do you see?

What has been your best career decision? Why?

What has been your worst career decision? Why?

What is the greatest career risk you've taken? What was the outcome?

What obstacles have prevented you from doing something with your career that you wanted?

Questions for Reflection (continued)

What portion of your lifeline has been influenced by others?

What would you do differently, if given the opportunity?

Look at the future events you've indicated on your lifeline. What are the three strongest career anchors? What pattern do you see?

What are your highest career goals and aspirations for the future?

What are your immediate plans for moving your career in the direction you want it to go?

You now have a better sense of your career progress and aspirations. By pinpointing the most significant influences thus far, you can begin to chart a path for your future. In the next section you'll identify your most important career values and examine the impact they'll have on future career decisions.

What is most important to you?

In the world of work today, we're faced with so many choices, from where we want to work to how we want to work. At times, you might feel overwhelmed by the number of life-changing choices with which you're faced. Fortunately, understanding of our most important values can make the decision-making process much easier.

Values often change over time. That's because your values are influenced by internal and external factors that also change over time, such as parental influence, environment, personality characteristics, and interests.

How do you identify a value? When you declare it publicly, choose it freely without pressure, choose it from among alternative options, choose it after considering the pros and cons, and act upon it consistently.

Exercising your values motivates you to act in certain ways and helps you make decisions that are consistent with those values, despite the circumstances. For example, if family life is your most important value, when you're faced with a decision that will impact the quality of your family life, such as working late to complete a project, you'll take that impact into account.

The exercise that follows is designed to help you clarify the values you hold today. By completing the checklist, you'll be better equipped to make future decisions based on values that are personally satisfying.

Fast Track Your Career: Three Steps for Finding Work You Love

Career Values Inventory

Step One: Read each value listed and put an X in the appropriate box based on importance to you.

	Very Important	Important	Average	Little Importance	No Importance
Security — Be assured of keeping my job with a reasonable expectation of financial reward					
Adventure — Have work duties that involve exciting or unusual experiences					
Stability — Have a predictable work routine and job duties					
Artistic Expression — Engage in creative work in any of several art forms					
Challenging Problems — Hold a position that provides opportunities to solve problems and avoid continual routine					
Help Others — Help people directly, either individually or in small groups					
Physical Activity — Move around often during the work day					
Work Under Pressure — Work in situations where time pressure is common and/or others judge quality of work critically					

Chapter Two - Find Meaning in Your Career

Fast Track Your Career: Three Steps for Finding Work You Love

	Very Important	Important	Average	Little Importance	No Importance
Independence — Be able to determine nature of work without much direction from others; not required to do what others tell me					
Supervision — Be directly responsible for work done by others					
Time Freedom — Accomplish tasks according to my own time schedule; no specific working hours required					
Intellectual Status — Be regarded as a person with high intellectual aptitude or an acknowledged expert in my field					
Knowledge — Engage myself in pursuit of knowledge, truth, and understanding					
Affiliation — Be associated with a particular organization, group, or community					
Location — Find a town or geographic area that is conducive to my lifestyle and affords an opportunity to enjoy things					
Work Alone — Do projects that allow me to work by myself, without much contact with others					

	Very Important	Important	Average	Little Importance	No Importance
Make Decisions — Have the power to make decisions on courses of action, policies, or procedures					
Advancement — The opportunity to work hard and make rapid career advancement					
Status — Friends, family and community respect my position					
High Earnings Anticipated — Monetary rewards that allow me to purchase the essentials and luxuries I want					
Creative Expression — Opportunity to express, in writing or verbally, my ideas concerning the job and how I might improve it					
Excitement — Experience high degree of (or frequent) excitement in the course of my work					
Public Contact — Have a lot of daily contact with people					
Recognition — Be recognized for the quality of my work in a visible or public way					

Fast Track Your Career: Three Steps for Finding Work You Love

	Very Important	Important	Average	Little Importance	No Importance
Personal Growth — Be able to pursue personal development					
Influence — in a position to sway the attitudes or opinions of other people					
Creativity — Create new ideas, programs, processes or business models following a format developed by others					
Exercise Competence — Opportunity to involve myself in areas in which I feel I have above-average talents and proficiency					
Fast Pace — Work in an environment where work must be done rapidly					
Profit, Gain — Opportunity for accumulating large amounts of money or other compensation through raises, commissions, or stock options					
Advance Knowledge — A) Be involved in hard science or human research, B) work in a company considered to be one of the best in its field and which strives for better product advances					

	Very Important	Important	Average	Little Importance	No Importance
Work With Others — Work as part of a team to achieve common goals					
Competition — Engage in activities that match my abilities against those of others					
Leadership — Manage work activities, operations or resources					
Change — Have work responsibilities that frequently change in content and setting					
Friendships — Develop close personal relationships with co-workers					
Help Society — Do something to contribute to the improvement of the world					
Moral Fulfillment — Feel that my work is contributing to moral standards that I feel are very important					
Aesthetics — Be involved in studying or appreciating the beauty of things, ideas, the environment and my surroundings					

Fast Track Your Career: Three Steps for Finding Work You Love

	Very Important	Important	Average	Little Importance	No Importance
Physical Challenge — Have a job that makes physical demands I would find rewarding					
Family — Have sufficient time to focus on my family					
Job Tranquility — To avoid pressures in my job function and work environment					
Routine — Have regular work hours					
Task Orientation — Systematically complete projects achieving well-defined standards					
Individuality — Feel open to express my uniqueness					
Autonomy — Have direct control over my time and responsibilities					
Environment — Work outdoors using my body or operating equipment					

Step Two: After marking your responses, list of all of the values you ranked as **Very Important** in the space below.

Step Three: Review your list of **Very Important** values. If you have more than 10 values listed, pare down your list.

Step Four: Arrange your list of **Very Important** values in priority order, with the most important value labeled as #1. List those values below.

Fast Track Your Career: Three Steps for Finding Work You Love

Questions for Reflection

Take some time to reflect on the values you selected in the Career Values Inventory by answering the questions in the space below.

What did you notice about your values selection?

Were you surprised by what you selected as your most important and least important values? If so, why?

Was it easy or hard for you to prioritize your values? Why?

In what ways are your most important values reflected in your career today?

In what ways would your career be enhanced if it incorporated your most important values?

In this chapter you clarified what is most important to you and how you'd like your values to be integrated into your life and career. Next, we'll take a look at your skills and the role they play in career satisfaction.

Discover What You're Good At

Excellence through Action

In all the work that you do, there is always an interaction among a combination of data, people, and things. Data skills deal with handling information. This includes taking in, processing, analyzing and giving out information. The information can be in the factual form of ideas, facts, and numbers, and experiential in the form of emotions, colors, and sounds. People skills involve interactions with people for various reasons. When you're using people skills you might be providing care, teaching, supervising, managing, counseling or helping. Thing skills are related to working with objects and physicality. Activities include building, constructing, filing, repairing, running, walking, and holding. It's useful to understand what type of skills you tend to use the most. That will give you some insight into where you tend to focus your attention, and perhaps uncover potential new career opportunities, whether it be a new project team at work, a new hobby, or a new career.

Skills can also be divided into three categories: functional/transferable (also referred to as portable), work-specific, and self-management skills. Functional/transferable skills can be applied in most environments and situations. They incorporate various combinations of data, people, and thing skills. Examples of functional skills include communication, planning, organizing, managing, analyzing, and problem-solving. Work-specific skills are specific to a job and are not easily applied in other environments or situations. These skills tend to be technical and specialized, for example, fixing a carburetor, performing surgery, and writing a computer software code. Self-management skills (sometimes referred to as personality traits) are related to how we conduct ourselves and are rooted in temperament. Examples of these skills include taking the initiative, resourcefulness, being good-natured, and reliability.

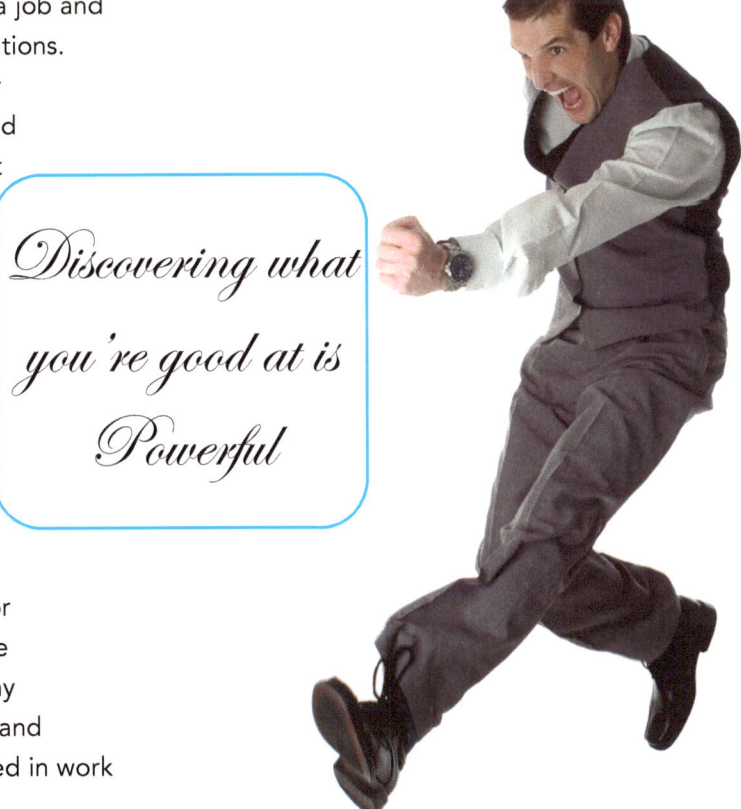

Discovering what you're good at is Powerful

What are you good at? The question is difficult to answer for many people. Quite often, it's taken for granted that everyone has the same abilities, and at the same level. That leads some people to assume that their abilities aren't unique or special in any way. Of course that's not the case. We all possess a set of skills that can be applied to many activities. For example, if you're a highly organized and planful person, you might find those skills being used in work situations such as event planning, and in your personal life when you plan parties, vacations and other leisure activities.

We each have different skill levels and preferences. When it comes to career satisfaction, what's most important is using your strongest and most enjoyable skills—what we call your "Motivated Skills [1]"—in a meaningful way.

What about those skills that you're weak in, but you enjoy using in your work? These are "Skills to Develop." As you work to improve those skills, you add more to your toolkit. You can enhance these skills by taking on new projects and assignments at work, volunteering, taking classes, and reading books.

On the other hand, skills you are good at but don't enjoy using can lead to burnout. Many people have built successful careers on these skills. It's no surprise then, that they spend a large part of their careers doing work they don't enjoy. If your skills fall into this category, you probably feel a sense of competence but don't feel as satisfied as you could. That means you're in the "Burnout Zone."

The grid below represents the skill areas.

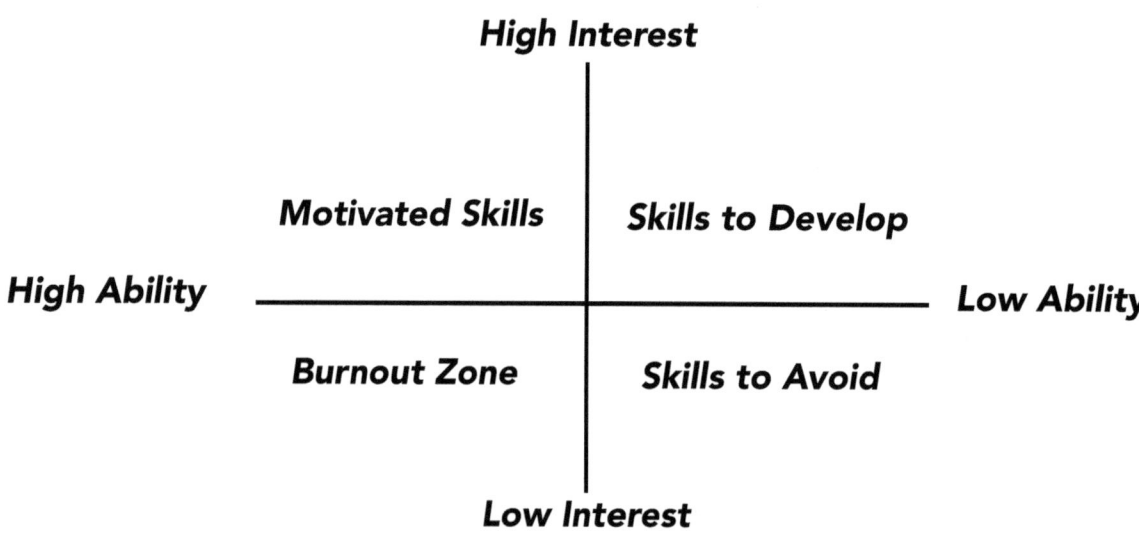

[1] *Knowdell, Richard (1996). Building a Career Development Program. Palo Alto, CA: Davies-Black.*

Fast Track Your Career: Three Steps for Finding Work You Love

It's important to keep in mind that employers evaluate potential employees based on certain skills and attributes. For example, employers seek employees who have demonstrated the ability to communicate effectively, work well with people (clients and co-workers), analyze information, solve problems, think creatively, provide leadership, and have technical competence.

The exercise that follows is the first step in identifying your Motivated Skills. It's also the foundation for generating accomplishment statements, which describe how you've successfully applied your skills. You'll be able to use the skills list to research aspects of jobs that you might enjoy.

Avoid burnout by using your "Motivated Skills"

Chapter Three - Discover What You're Good At **29**

Skills Inventory

Step One: Put a ✔ next to the skills on this list that you feel you possess. Feel free to add other skills that are not on the list.

Administration	Advise	Advocate	Allocate
Assemble	Act as liaison	Analyze	Appraise
Arbitrate	Artistic ability	Assign	Athletic
Budget	Build	Calculate	Care for animals
Categorize	Clarify	Classify	Coach
Collect Data	Communicate	Compile	Compose music
Compute	Concentrate	Conceptualize	Construct
Coordinate	Counsel	Count	Create
Creative expression	Critique	Cultivate	Delegate
Decide	Design	Detail	Develop
Diagnose	Direct	Display	Draw
Edit	Educate	Encourage	Enforce
Entertain	Establish	Estimate	Examine
Expedite	Evaluate	Facilitate	File documents
Fix	Follow through	Gather	Generate ideas
Guide	Help	Host, Hostess	Implement
Influence	Inform	Initiate	Innovate
Inspect	Interpret	Interview	Invent
Investigate	Keep records	Lead	Listen
Make arrangements	Make decisions	Manage	Manage projects
Manage people	Manual dexterity	Market	Mathematical ability
Mechanical ability	Meet deadlines	Mediate	Monitor
Motivate	Musical ability	Negotiate	Nurse
Observe	Operate equipment	Organize	Perform
Persuade	Physical coordination	Plan	Plant
Play music	Prepare food	Prioritize	Process
Produce crafts	Promote	Proofread	Provide hospitality
Read for comprehension	Reason	Recommend	Repair
Research	Review	Schedule	Sell
Social	Solve problems	Speak in public	Statistical analysis
Survey	Synthesize	Systematize	Supervise
Teach	Test	Train	Transport
Treat	Use computers	Use equipment	Use imagination
Use intuition	Use tools	Validate	Visualize
Work with hands	Write		

Step Two: Put an X next to the skills on the list that you do, or would enjoy using the most.

Step Three: Put a — next to the skills on the list that you do not or would not enjoy using.

Step Four: List the skills that you marked with both a ✔ and X on the lines below. These are your "Motivated Skills." When considering future projects, assignments or career opportunities, you'll want to make sure that these skills are a big part of your daily job responsibilities. You excel at them and get satisfaction from using them.

In what ways are you using your motivated skills in your current job?

Step Five: List the skills that you marked with an X. These are "Skills to Develop." When considering future projects, assignments or career opportunities, you'll want to seek out opportunities to enhance these skills.

In what specific ways can you develop or improve those skills?

Step Six: List the skills that you marked with a —. These are in the "Skills to Avoid." When considering future projects, assignments or career opportunities, you'll want to make sure that these skills are only supportive to your Motivated Skills and not part of your primary job responsibilities.

If necessary, in what specific ways can you reorganize your current assignments so that you're using fewer of these skills?

Step Seven: List the skills that you marked with a ✔ and a —. These are in the "Burnout Zone." When considering future projects, assignments or career opportunities, you'll want to avoid these skills.

If necessary, in what specific ways can you reorganize your current assignments so that you're using fewer of these skills?

You now know what you're good at and the skills you most enjoy using. Next, you'll summarize the exercises you've completed so far and create a **Career Self-Assessment Summary.** You can use this summary as reference as you identify next steps and explore career possibilities.

Career Self-Assessment Summary

When I was in that management development course years ago, I had the opportunity to map out my career goals and aspirations. I had completed several exercises and career assessments as you have just done and then summarized them into my dream career. That was a powerful exercise for two reasons: 1) I realized that what I wanted to accomplish couldn't be done in the organization where I worked, and 2) I had a clear vision of what I did want to accomplish and why. It was at that point I could begin planning for my future career.

In preparation for creating your Ideal Career Path, summarize the exercises you have completed so far.

Briefly describe your career path to date

List Your Top 3 Career Anchors

List Your Top 10 Career Values

List Your Motivated Skills

List Skills to Develop

Ideal Career Path

To set the stage for planning a satisfying career, you're going to design your Ideal Career Path. In as much detail as possible, describe the kind of work you're doing and where you're working (setting, environment, geographic location). Describe the people with whom you're working, how much money you make and the benefits you earn. Describe what you'll be doing in six months, one year, five years, and ten years. Design your Ideal Career Path as if there are no limitations. Be generous with your description. Don't worry if you aren't completely clear at this point. This is a process. Over time your path will crystallize.

Ideal Career Path

In this part of the career guide you completed a series of exercises that gave you insight into your unique attributes. You're now ready to begin exploring your career possibilities.

PART TWO

GETTING A REALITY CHECK

Fast Track Your Career: Three Steps for Finding Work You Love

Find Good Career Information

Uncovering Real Opportunities

Before you decide to pursue a particular career path, you need a reality check to determine which careers will meet your specific needs, based on the elements of your Career Self-Assessment Summary. For example, say you're interested in becoming a marketing professional because you want a job that will let you indulge your creativity, give you an opportunity to work on interesting projects, and allow you to work on a flexible schedule. But will a marketing job really meet all of those requirements?

In this chapter we'll explore how to research careers so that you can answer critical questions like that. You'll learn how to find your ideal work environment, co-workers who share your interests, skills, values, and personality traits; what industries and employers have positions for people with your skills and education; and how to locate opportunities based on your geographic preferences. As you learn more about various careers, it will be easier to identify which options meet your needs. You might discover that because you enjoy variety and challenge, a small company where you can perform many roles is a better option than a large company that places a higher value on specialized performance.

It's while conducting career information research that you test your assumptions about career possibilities, the world of work, and uncover real opportunities. You also have the chance to begin building a professional network which will be integral to your career advancement.

Test your assumptions… and uncover real opportunities

Chapter Four - Find Good Career Information 37

How do I know which careers to research?

When you began this career guide, you may have already had some ideas about careers you'd like to pursue. By now you might have expanded your list of options.

In this section I'll walk you through a series of steps to generate a list of potential careers to pursue. You'll be using several methods and resources such as the Internet, books, magazines, conferences, professional association meetings, and colleagues. You'll become familiar with a variety of careers and aspects of jobs, identify potential employers, learn about industries and job outlooks. When you're done, you'll be equipped to make sound decisions about your career choices.

Refer back to your Career Self-Assessment Summary, which contains a list of careers based on your interest patterns. The website **O*Net Online** (http://online.onetcenter.org/) has a search feature you can use to search for careers by keyword. Using the search feature on the site, you can generate a list of careers based on skills, job families, and industries. Simply type in the combination of attributes, and a list of relevant careers will appear. Select the careers that you would like to learn more about.

Keep an eye out for careers that appear in multiple searches. For example, if after searching for options based on interests and skills you come up with marketing manager, public relations coordinator, and event planner, you might want to put them on your list to research.

For further assistance, refer to **The Occupational Outlook Handbook** (http://www.bls.gov/oco/home.htm). It contains a section called "related occupations." You can search for careers you are interested in and refer to the "related occupations" section to identify more jobs to research.

List the careers you'll research in the space below:

Where do I get reliable information about the specific careers that interest me?

Before you move forward, you need objective information such as job outlook, potential employers, job attributes, salary levels, job functions, entry and advancement options, environments, and related occupations. It's equally important to get first-hand accounts from people who are actually doing the jobs in which you're interested. All of this input will give you a more balanced view of the world of work and will foster important professional relationships. You'll get exposed to different work environments, learn how people advance in various careers, and gain insight into their daily activities.

As you research the options, keep in mind that you need to answer specific questions:

- What are the duties and tasks of this occupation?
- What are the typical skills necessary?
- What educational background and other qualifications are required? What graduate degree or additional education will be required for advancement?
- What are some of the benefits/rewards of this type of career? (i.e. salary, career advancement, job security, future employment outlook, etc.)
- What are some occupations related to this field?
- Where can I find additional information about this career? (i.e. professional associations, trade magazines, internet resources, library resources, etc.)

Online and Print Resources

The Internet is a powerful tool for researching careers. As mentioned above, for preliminary research refer to the online edition of the **Occupational Outlook Handbook** (http://www.bls.gov/oco/home.htm) and **O*Net Online** (http://online.onetcenter.org/). Both resources provide information on hundreds of jobs and describe the training and education needed, earnings, job outlook, what workers do on the job, and working conditions. They also provide links to related occupations and relevant professional associations.

Researching Job Outlook and Industry Information

Attending professional association meetings, conferences and events is a great way to learn about industry trends and job opportunities. You can learn about growth in the industry, emerging opportunities and potential employers in your region.

The Encyclopedia of Associations is a directory that lists associations for every interest, hobby, profession, and industry. Most libraries carry a copy in their reference section. You can also search Yahoo! or Google to find online listings of associations. Look for regional chapters that hold events in your area.

For information on industries, you can review the **Occupational Outlook Quarterly** - http://www.bls.gov/opub/ooq/ooqhome.htm and **America's Career InfoNet** - http://www.careerinfonet.org/

Informational Interviews

People love to talk about what they do and are excellent sources of career information. You can talk with people in your company, outside your company, or within your profession. A technique that is often used is **"informational interviewing."** It involves setting an appointment to talk with someone about their job, career, and company so that you have an insider's perspective. During these interviews you can also get tips on the best ways to get started, where to look for jobs, how to get access to the hidden job market, how to get referrals, and how to expand your professional network.

An in-person informational interview is best, but if the only way you can get personal accounts about job experiences is via phone, that's fine, too. To get the most value from informational interviewing, seek out professionals who work in different environments. If you're considering teaching, for example, talk with teachers in public-school and private-school settings. If you're interested in marketing, talk with marketing professionals in corporate, academic, and agency settings.

Do some preparation before your informational interview. First, be as clear as possible about your career aspirations. Then, decide what you really want to know about the job, and formulate relevant questions. Treat the meeting as a professional interview and dress in appropriate business attire. True, it's not a job interview, but you're still being evaluated so you want to make the best impression possible. Finally, research the company by visiting its website or reading press releases and annual reports. You want to show some interest, knowledge, and enthusiasm. I've provided a sample list of questions at the end of the chapter.

Identify 10-15 career possibilities. Then start looking for people to interview. The easiest way to find them is to search your address book for people you already know. You can also ask friends, colleagues, instructors, and advisors if they know anyone in your target professions, and if they would be willing to make an introduction. If these measures don't work, ask for referrals from your college's alumni association, professional associations, and community organizations.

Once you have identified people to interview, contact them to introduce yourself and request a meeting. Most people are very comfortable being contacted via e-mail, especially if they're frequent business travelers. However, it's always a nice touch to send a personalized, handwritten letter, and follow it up with a phone call or e-mail.

Below are sample letters of introduction:

Situation - Referred by Colleague

> Dear Mr. Jones,
>
> Your colleague, Joe Smith, suggested I contact you. I am currently a project manager at The Big Corporation. I am interested in obtaining a similar position in a smaller company, and Joe thought you might be willing to share your insight on different aspects of the field.
>
> If your schedule permits, I would like to schedule an office visit in the next two weeks. I am available to speak by telephone, if you prefer.
>
> Thank you for your consideration. I look forward to speaking with you soon.
>
> Sincerely,
>
> *Scott Seeker*

Situation - No Referral

> Dear Mrs. Johnson,
>
> I found your contact information while researching career information on the Global Marketing Today website. I am currently doing research on marketing careers and am interviewing several professionals in different settings. I would appreciate talking with you about your experiences as a marketing professional.
>
> If your schedule permits, I would like to schedule an office visit in the next two weeks. I am available to speak by telephone, if you prefer.
>
> Thank you for your consideration. I look forward to speaking with you soon.
>
> Sincerely,
>
> *Carla Curious*

Sample Questions for Your Informational Interview:

What is a typical day like?

How do you spend most of your time at work?

How did you decide to pursue this career path? What other careers were you considering?

What career advancement opportunities do you see in this industry?

What trends are impacting opportunities in this field?

What advice would you offer to someone considering this career path?

In what professional associations are you active?

What is the most rewarding part of your career?

What is the culture like in this company?

How are people typically promoted in your company?

Can you give me an example of entry-level opportunities in this field?

What kind of education and experience is typically needed to enter this field?

Following the informational interviews, it's important to follow up by sending a handwritten thank you note. Again, depending on circumstances, you may have to send your thank you via e-mail. If the person you've interviewed suggested additional resources or made a referral, report back to him or her that you followed through on the information. Once you've decided on a career path to pursue, it's also a nice gesture to update the people you've interviewed and thank them again for their insight.

You now have the skills for determining what will bring you satisfaction in your career and how to find the best opportunities. There are many strategies for advancing your career. In the next chapter we'll look at the most common and effective techniques for moving forward.

Fast Track Your Career: Three Steps for Finding Work You Love

PART THREE

CHARTING YOUR CAREER PATH

Fast Track Your Career: Three Steps for Finding Work You Love

Learn How To Get Ahead

Chapter 5

Keys to Success

You're now ready to apply what you've learned. There are many strategies for successfully navigating the world of work. Whether you're climbing the corporate ladder or working for the common good, the same strategies apply. Successful professionals consistently evaluate their career progress, manage their relationships, engage in life-long learning, gain visibility through professional involvement, develop leadership skills, and work toward achieving long-term goals. This section will give you an overview of the many ways you can advance your career.

Ongoing Evaluation and Self-Assessment

In Chapter Two I discussed how career aspirations can shift as you move through various life stages.

At certain points throughout your work life, you'll find yourself evaluating your career. These evaluations can re-invigorate a stagnant career, re-focus a derailed career, or inspire you to re-commit to a previously satisfying career. The evaluations can also propel you toward more rapid advancement. While not everyone strives to climb the corporate ladder, it's safe to assume that most of us want to at least enjoy positive work experiences most of the time. After becoming competent in your profession, your colleagues and managers take for granted that you can perform consistently at acceptable levels. Once you've reached that point, a shift occurs. It's no longer enough to show up and do a good job. You're now being evaluated on how well you get along with others. Managing key relationships in the workplace and your profession become the focal point. Whether you want to advance or just be happy at work, the way you manage your relationship with your bosses, co-workers and employees will have a big impact.

Relationships are the key

Building Professional Relationships

While managing your functional work relationships is important, so too is building a network of people you can call on in various situations. These people will come in many forms and take on many roles. You need to become adept at managing relationships with people at all levels of the organization, including your boss, your peers, and the people you manage.

Your network should include:
- Mentors who provide career guidance, access to opportunities, and access to information
- Role Models who demonstrate behaviors and attributes that you admire
- Challengers who provide critical feedback for improvement
- Promoters who keep you informed of opportunities and encourage your visibility

Some people may fall into one or more categories, but you shouldn't rely on only a handful of people to meet your professional relationship needs. Having a broad, in-depth network will help safeguard your career from the inevitable peaks and valleys. You can meet people at work and in a variety of other situations, including serving on a board of directors, conference committees, ad hoc committees, intra-office involvement, and special events.

Continuing Your Education and Training

In certain career areas, you can't progress without advanced degrees, certification, and education. Even if you aren't aiming for a job promotion, you may continue to advance your education, either formally or informally. Many professionals also find it valuable to learn new skills and pursue their interests. You'll find that pursuing professional education will naturally expand your professional network. There are many ways to continue your education, including taking classes, as well as attending workshops, seminars, and conferences.

Gaining Visibility through Professional Involvement

A great way to help advance your career is to become involved in professional organizations and company activities. Both are sources for professional contacts and help you stay up-to-date on industry trends. In addition, many professional organizations offer opportunities to showcase your knowledge by taking on leadership roles or speaking to members. They also offer specialized, industry-specific training.

Developing Your Leadership Skills

All employers are looking for leadership qualities. They place a high value on their employees' ability to communicate a clear vision, establish and implement plans effectively, create and work to budget, raise funds, and negotiate. Leadership qualities are such an important criteria for advancement, it would be to your career advantage to develop those skills. The workplace and community offer many built-in opportunities to learn them. You can get involved in helping to manage cross-functional projects, serve on internal improvement committees, and participate on advisory boards.

Planning for Future Career Opportunities

As you look ahead, think of strategies that will help you gain the experience and develop the skills that you'll need to move your career to the next level. Start by answering the following questions:
- What can I do to foster, maintain, and enhance my professional relationships?
- How will I keep my knowledge up to date?
- How will I gain visibility through professional involvement?
- How will I develop my leadership skills?

You have now gained personal insight, learned how to find useful career information and learned several strategies to advance your career. In the next chapter, we'll put that all together and look at a proven technique for goal-setting.

Setting goals motivates you to acheive

Plan for Next Steps

What's Next?
S.M.A.R.T. Goal-setting

Every day, you have new experiences, learn something new, and meet new people that change the way you see and do things. Along the way, you make decisions based on your core values. The goals you decide to pursue are a reflection of what you need and want, what you hold near and dear, and what will bring you satisfaction and fulfillment. If you don't work to set and achieve your goals, you're ignoring a very important part of your psyche. Goals express what you feel is important to accomplish, and there may be more than one way to reach your goals. It's important to keep in mind that while your goals often change, the essence of your goals - your core values - rarely change.

The goals you set for yourself are influenced by several factors, including your desire or passion in life and work, seen or unseen obstacles, risk tolerance, and the course or 'steps' you set to get there. They motivate you toward achievement, which is the building block for self-confidence. Whether consciously or not, we set goals using a general process.

While you may understand why it's important to actively set and work toward goals, it can be difficult to establish long-range goals. Why? You might feel that you have too much to lose, or your goals just seem too far away. That is why it's so important to pick short-term targets. It's much easier to break down your goals into manageable chunks and build on your successes.

As you begin to make small strides toward accomplishing your goals you'll be more motivated to go for the gold. The SMART method is a useful framework for setting manageable goals.

> **GOAL-SETTING PROCESS**
>
> **Define Goal** – determine what is to be accomplished
>
> **Assess Alternatives** – brainstorm possible ways the goal can be accomplished
>
> **Gather Information** – research options
>
> **Assess Outcome Probability and Desirability** – weigh the pros/cons and identify possible obstacles
>
> **Take Action** – do something!
>
> **Refine Goal** – evaluate, regroup and change course, if necessary

S.M.A.R.T. goals are Specific, Measurable, Achievable, Realistic, Time-framed

Let's take a closer look at these characteristics.

Specific — A goal must include important details about what you want to happen and how you are going to do it.

Goal — I want to lose weight.
SMART goal — I want to lose fifteen pounds.

Measurable — A goal must define measurable results so progress can be tracked.

Goal — I want to increase sales.
SMART goal — I will increase sales by 20%.

Attainable — A goal must be attainable within parameters over which you have control.

Goal — I want to lose fifteen pounds in two months.
SMART goal — I will lose fifteen pounds in six months by walking forty minutes, three times per week.

Realistic — A goal must be achievable with some effort, but not require going beyond what is reasonable.

Goal — I want to improve my presentation skills for upcoming speaking engagements.
SMART goal — I will improve my presentation skills by practicing regularly and joining Toastmasters.

Time-framed — A goal must have a deadline for accomplishment.

Goal — I want to complete my certificate in general management.
SMART goal — I'll complete my certificate in general management in the Spring semester.

SMART Goal-setting

Setting good goals and planning how you'll reach those goals is a great way to take control of your life. They also allow you to channel your energy toward your purpose.

In the exercise that follows, you will apply the technique to help you set a goal that is SMART.

Step One: Refer to your **Career Lifeline** in which you selected some short-term and long-term milestones. Select one career goal to work with.

Step Two: Write a statement about how you'll achieve this career goal in the space below.

Step Three: Rewrite the statement applying the SMART method in the space below.

In the final chapter of this career guide you'll establish an action plan for achieving your career goals. By applying the techniques to your personal situation, you will be on the way to turning your dreams into reality!

Plan to Succeed

Personal Career Action Plan

Now it's time for you to take the long view of your career. Where do you see yourself in the future? In the previous chapters, you created your Ideal Career Path, learned about how people advance in their careers, how to set goals, and how to plan action steps for achieving them using the SMART method.

In the following exercise you'll use the SMART method for goal setting to plan your career's next steps. Below are some questions to help you formulate your immediate, intermediate, and long-term goals.

- Given what you know about how people in your profession advance and manage their careers, what do you need to do?

- What obstacles do you foresee?

- What resources are available to you?

- What people do you already know who can help you?

- Who do you need to meet?

- What assignments or experiences do you need to achieve your goal?

Refer back to your **Ideal Career Path** from Chapter Three. In the spaces below, describe in as much detail as possible, your six-month, one-year, and five-year goals. Then, outline the specific steps you'll take to achieve your goals. I've provided some guidelines to get you started, but you should expand your descriptions so you have something to work with.

Within six months, I'll be at this point in my career (describe in detail)

Desired position:

Desired company(s):

Desired geographic region:

Desired salary, benefits and other compensation:

I know the following people who can help get me connected to opportunities in that company/organization:

I'll contact them via letter, e-mail or phone call by (date):

I'll introduce myself to the following people who can help get me connected to career opportunities:

I'll use the following job search resources:

I'll check for job openings every (select week day):

I'll follow up by telephone or email every (select week day):

Some Suggested Activities: 1) Identify employment resources and select companies that have appropriate position openings. 2) Select appropriate educational programs. 3) Select relevant professional associations and become involved. 4) Create an effective resume, cover letter and other support materials. 5) Fine-tune your interviewing and networking skills. 6) Get organized and follow up.

Use a calendar to plan your job search and career advancement activities for six months.

In one year, I'll be at this point in my career (describe in detail)

Desired position:

Desired company:

Desired geographic region:

Desired salary, benefits and other compensation:

Desired lifestyle:

Planned continuing education (certification, education, training):

Planned professional involvement:

Between now and one year, I'll do the following to meet my goals
Action Steps:

In five years, I'll be at this point in my career (describe in detail)

Desired position:

Desired company:

Desired geographic region:

Desired salary, benefits and other compensation:

Desired lifestyle:

Planned continuing education (certification, education, training):

Planned professional involvement:

Between now and five years, I'll do the following to meet my goals
Action Steps:

Year One

Year Two

Year Three

Year Four

Year Five

Some Suggested Activities: 1) Select appropriate educational programs and relevant professional associations and become involved. 2) Update your resume/CV, cover letter and other support materials. 3) Brush-up on your interviewing and networking skills. 4) Get organized and follow up. 5) Find mentors and expand your professional network.

Now that you've got the skills, it's full speed ahead

As you move forward in your career, you'll have your Personal Career Action Plan as a guide to managing your career and life. By completing the exercises in this career guide, you've developed the evaluation and decision-making skills you'll need throughout your career. You can now make the best decisions based on your values, interests, personality traits, motivated skills, and goals. To ensure that you're always moving in a satisfying direction, periodically evaluate your career progress and update the goals and action steps in your Personal Career Action Plan. Don't forget to capture your successes and key accomplishments, too!

A Few Concluding Thoughts

If you've completed the exercises in this career guide, I congratulate you! You've started on the journey toward career satisfaction. You've re-evaluated your most important values and how they impact your career satisfaction. You've identified what motivates you to do your best. You've uncovered your motivated skills, areas for skill enhancement, and areas to avoid.

Your **Career Action Plan** will guide you as you travel down the path toward a career that you love.

Are you still working your way through the exercises? I encourage you to forge ahead. Once you complete the exercises, you'll be armed with knowledge and a boost in confidence that will help you find a career that you love.

Career Information Resources

If you're still struggling to get clarity about where to start, I recommend the following resources.

Career-planning Books

Do What You Are by Tieger and Barron-Tieger

I Could Do Anything If Only I Knew What It Was by Barbara Sher

Second Acts by Stephen Pollan

What Color is Your Parachute by Richard Bolles

Do What You Love, the Money Will Follow by Marsha Sinetar

The Psychology of Careers, Donald Super

Now! Discover Your Strengths by Marcus Buckingham

Follow Your True Colors to The Work You Love by Carolyn Kalil

Real People, Real Jobs by Montross, Leibowitz, and Shinkman

Up Is Not The Only Way by Beverly Kaye

Personal Development Books

Passages and New Passages Gail Sheehy

The Seasons of a Man's Life, Daniel J. Levinson

The Psychology of Careers, Donald Super

Self Matters by Philip C. McGraw, Ph.D.

Online Career Information Links

O*Net Center — http://online.onetcenter.org

America's Career InfoNet — http://www.acinet.org/acinet

What You Need To Know About Career Planning — http://careerplanning.about.com

Monster Career Advice — http://content.monster.com

Occupational Outlook Handbook — http://www.bls.gov/oco/

The Riley Guide — http://www.rileyguide.com

About Futures in Motion, Inc.

At Futures in Motion, Inc. we believe you shouldn't just work at a job — you should thrive at it! Whether you want advancement within the framework of your current career or whether you want to make a transition to a new industry, a new organization or a new position, we can help you with:

- Assessing your unique interests, strengths, values and personality traits
- Researching careers that have the greatest potential to give you the best fit and satisfaction
- Preparing personal marketing materials such as resumes and cover letters
- Researching industries and organizations to generate more opportunities than you are currently aware of
- Mapping out a step-by-step strategy for landing the job of your dreams
- Coaching to support you throughout the process.

Our services include online career assessment, career counseling and coaching, teleclasses, and resume writing.

Contact Us Now!

Get your career in focus and reclaim your passion for work. Contact Markell today to schedule a complimentary, 20-minute career consultation. She can be reached at markell@futures-in-motion.com or (877) 210-3252.
www.futures-in-motion.com

About the Author

Markell R. Steele, M.Ed.

Markell Steele is the owner and principal career counselor for Futures in Motion, Inc. She oversees all aspects of delivering comprehensive career management services to managers and executives nationwide. Her services include career counseling and coaching, executive and leadership coaching, business development, marketing, strategy development and general management.

Markell works directly with clients to help them develop the tools they need to create and manage satisfying careers. She is an expert in the career management process and provides her clients with a wealth of knowledge about the world of work and strategies for career success. As a counselor and coach, she facilitates career decision-making, job search action planning, self-marketing campaign development, professional network development, and leadership development. In addition to working with individual clients, Markell's company also provides career and executive coaching services to the UCLA Anderson Executive Program participants, UCLA Anderson FEMBA/EMBA Alumni, and Readyminds, Inc.

For more than eight years, Markell taught classes on the topics of career motivation and success, career assessment, career exploration, effective job search strategies, and career transition for adults evaluating their career paths. She has taught for the Learning Annex in Los Angeles and as an adjunct instructor at Fullerton College.

Markell received a Master of Education degree in Counseling from the University of San Diego (USD) and a Bachelor of Arts degree in Sociology from the University of California, Santa Barbara (UCSB). She is a National Certified Counselor and among the first career counselors nationwide to become a Distanced Credentialed Counselor.

Markell is the Director of Education for NAWBO-OC (National Association of Women Business Owners) and was recognized as the chapter's Member of the Year for 2006. She is also a board member for the UCSB Alumni Association. She is an active volunteer for UCSB Alumni Association - Orange County Chapter, UCSB and UCLA Alumni Career Services.

Notes

www.ingramcontent.com/pod-product-compliance
Lightning Source LLC
Chambersburg PA
CBHW041538220426
43663CB00002B/71